REBEL
MOON
XXXTENTACION'S

Journey Against the World

A Story by LARTX

Contents

CONCLUSION

THE DUALITY OF XXXTENTACION

In the labyrinthine journey of XXXTentacion, we encounter a life marked by stark dualities—an individual whose existence was a continuous struggle between inner demons and the quest for redemption.

On one hand, Jahseh Onfroy's life was punctuated by turbulence and conflict, a young man wrestling with profound personal battles.

On the other, he was an artist who shattered conventions and defied expectations, pushing the boundaries of music and self-expression with an intensity that both captivated and alienated.

His journey reveals a portrait of a troubled soul seeking solace and meaning, grappling with a world that often seemed at odds with his very essence.

XXXTentacion's art was not just a reflection of his experiences but a defiant assertion of his identity, a beacon of his resilience amidst the chaos.

The controversial nature of his life and career only underscores the complexity of his existence—a poignant reminder of the human condition's capacity for both greatness and folly.

As we reflect on his legacy, it becomes clear that XXXTentacion's story is one of profound complexity, marked by the constant push and pull of redemption and rebellion.

His life, though fraught with conflict, serves as a powerful narrative about the multifaceted nature of human experience.

It is a testament to the struggle to carve out a place in a world that often fails to understand, yet ultimately offers a compelling exploration of resilience, vulnerability, and the relentless pursuit of self-discovery.

CHAPTER 1

THE GENESIS OF A REBEL

The world had always been a complicated place for Jahseh Onfroy. Born into a life of uncertainty and chaos, he quickly learned that survival required more than just strength—it demanded resilience, cunning, and a heart hardened by the harsh realities that surrounded him.

As a child, Jahseh was like any other, filled with dreams that glittered with innocence. But the streets of Broward County, Florida, had a way of stripping that innocence away.

His mother, often absent, was a fleeting presence in his life, and his father—a ghostly figure of what could have been—disappeared into the void of the prison system before Jahseh had the chance to know him.

The streets became his guide, the pulse of the neighborhood his teacher, and survival became his primary lesson.

In school, Jahseh found himself at odds with authority, constantly questioning the rules that sought to confine him. Teachers labeled him a troublemaker, a child too wild to be tamed.

But Jahseh wasn't just rebelling for the sake of rebellion; he was searching for something—an identity, a purpose, a way to make sense of a world that seemed intent on breaking him.

Music was his refuge, a world where his thoughts, raw and unfiltered, could find expression. The sound of a bass-heavy beat, the rhythm of a haunting melody—these were the tools he used to carve out his own space in a world that often felt too small.

He wasn't content to follow in anyone else's footsteps; he was determined to create his own path, no matter how treacherous it might be.

By the time he was a teenager, Jahseh had become XXXTentacion—a name that would soon resonate far beyond the walls of his small room, echoing through the digital corridors of SoundCloud and into the ears of thousands who, like him, felt out of place in the world. But the road to becoming XXXTentacion was not paved with gold; it was lined with the broken pieces of a young man's shattered dreams and the relentless pursuit of something more.

As his music began to gain traction, so did the controversies that would come to define much of his public persona. Arrests, fights, accusations—all became part of the narrative that the world would see. But behind the headlines and the viral clips, there was a boy still searching, still trying to find where he belonged.

Jahseh Onfroy was a contradiction, a young man filled with anger and love, violence and peace, despair and hope. The world saw him as a rebel, a troublemaker who refused to conform. But those who listened closely, who heard the pain in his lyrics and the vulnerability in his voice, knew there was more to his story.

And so, with every beat and every lyric, Jahseh began to write his own story—a story not just of rebellion, but of resilience, of survival, and of a relentless quest to be understood in a world that seemed intent on misunderstanding him.

The nights in Lauderhill were thick with humidity, the air so heavy it felt like it could crush you if you stood still too long. But Jahseh never stood still—his mind raced even when his body didn't, chasing after thoughts that never quite let him rest. The apartment he shared with his grandmother was a place of refuge and tension, a small space where the weight of his thoughts pressed against the thin walls.

Music was his only escape. With a cheap microphone and a borrowed laptop, Jahseh transformed his room into a makeshift studio. It wasn't much, but it was enough. He'd stay up late, the glow of the screen the only light in the room, pouring his soul into every track. His voice, a blend of raw emotion and relentless energy, filled the room and spilled out into the night.

The beats were rough, the lyrics rougher—honest to a fault, unpolished but undeniably real. He rapped about pain, about loss, about the anger that seemed to simmer just beneath the surface of his skin. But there was more than just rage in his music; there was a vulnerability that caught people off guard, a sense of longing that cut through the bravado.

It wasn't long before others started to notice. In the crowded, competitive world of SoundCloud rap, Jahseh's music stood out.

It wasn't just the sound—it was the emotion, the intensity, the feeling that every track was a glimpse into a mind that refused to be silenced.

He wasn't just making music; he was telling his story, and it was a story that resonated with anyone who had ever felt alone, misunderstood, or out of place.

But as his following grew, so did the shadows that seemed to follow him everywhere.

Fame came with a price, and for Jahseh, that price was steep.

The streets that had once been his home now felt like a trap, and the people who claimed to be his friends were often the first to betray him.

Trust was a luxury he couldn't afford, and paranoia became his constant companion.

Despite the mounting pressures, Jahseh pushed forward, driven by something he couldn't quite name. It wasn't just about making music—it was about proving something, to himself and to the world. He wanted to be seen, to be heard, to be understood, even as he struggled to understand himself.

The world outside might have been unforgiving, but inside his music, Jahseh found a way to confront the demons that haunted him. Each song was a battle, each lyric a weapon in his fight against the darkness. And though he knew the odds were stacked against him, he refused to back down.

For Jahseh, every day was a fight to stay afloat, to keep the darkness at bay. But in those moments when the music flowed, when the beats and the words came together just right, he felt something that resembled peace—a fleeting glimpse of what could be, if only the world would let him be.

But the world had other plans, and Jahseh knew it. He wasn't just fighting against the world—he was fighting against time, against fate, against the inevitable. And deep down, he knew that one day, the fight would come to an end.

But until that day came, Jahseh Onfroy—XXXTentacion— would continue to do what he did best: fight, create, and carve out his place in a world that seemed determined to push him aside.

CHAPTER 2

RISING AGAINST THE ODDS

The moon hung low in the night sky, casting a pale, ghostly glow over the streets below. It was a reminder of the darkness that lingered, but also of the light that could break through—even if only for a moment. Jahseh often found himself staring at that moon, feeling its pull, as if it understood the turmoil churning inside him.

With every step he took in the world of music, the stakes grew higher. The underground scene had its own rules, its own hierarchy, and Jahseh wasn't content to play by anyone's rules but his own. He had something to prove, not just to the world, but to himself.

His breakthrough came in the form of a track that was as raw and unfiltered as the emotions that fueled it. "Look at Me!" was a sonic explosion—a chaotic blend of distorted bass, aggressive lyrics, and a delivery that demanded attention. It was unlike anything that had come before it, a track that defied convention and resonated with a generation that was tired of the same old sound.

The song spread like wildfire, igniting a movement that no one saw coming. Jahseh wasn't just another SoundCloud rapper—he was a force, a voice for the voiceless, a reflection of the anger and frustration that so many young people felt. The world began to take notice, and with that attention came everything Jahseh had both hoped for and feared.

As "Look at Me!" climbed the charts, the media couldn't ignore the young man behind the track. But they didn't just see an artist—they saw a target.

Jahseh's past, filled with brushes with the law, personal demons, and controversies, became fodder for headlines that painted him as a villain. The more his music spread, the more the world tried to box him in, to define him by his mistakes rather than his potential.

But Jahseh was more than the sum of his parts, and he refused to be caged by the world's expectations.

He knew he had a choice: to let the weight of the world crush him, or to rise above it, to push back and carve out his destiny.

It wasn't an easy path, but then again, nothing in his life had ever been easy.

He doubled down on his music, channeling every ounce of pain, anger, and defiance into his work.

His next projects were a testament to his complexity—songs that were as haunting as they were powerful, lyrics that spoke to his inner battles as well as the struggles of those who listened.

Tracks like "Jocelyn Flores" and "Revenge" revealed a side of Jahseh that many hadn't seen before—a young man grappling with loss, and guilt, with the desire to make things right even as the world seemed to conspire against him.

But success brought new challenges. The world watched his every move, waiting for him to slip, to fall back into the patterns that had once defined him.

Jahseh felt the pressure, the weight of expectations from fans who saw him as a savior, and from critics who saw him as a ticking time bomb.

In the midst of it all, Jahseh found himself increasingly isolated. Fame had a way of creating distance—between him and the people he once trusted, between him and the life he had known.

He sought solace in the moonlit nights, where he could think, where he could breathe, where the world couldn't reach him.

But the moonlight couldn't shield him from everything. The shadows that had always been there, lurking in the corners of his mind, seemed to grow darker with each passing day. The pressure, the expectations, the weight of his own ambitions—it all began to take its toll.

Yet, even as the odds stacked against him, Jahseh refused to back down.

He knew that his journey was far from over, that there was still so much he needed to say, so much he needed to prove.

The world might have been against him, but he had learned to rise above it, to push forward even when everything seemed to be pulling him back.

Jahseh Onfroy was not just fighting for himself; he was fighting for everyone who had ever felt like the world was against them, for everyone who had ever stared up at the moon and wondered if they'd ever find their place in the darkness.

And so, under that same moon that had watched over him since he was a child, Jahseh continued to rise, against the odds, against the world, and against the shadows that threatened to consume him.

Jahseh Onfroy was not just fighting for himself; he was fighting for everyone who had ever felt like the world was against them, for everyone who had ever stared up at the moon and wondered if they'd ever find their place in the darkness.

And so, under that same moon that had watched over him since he was a child, Jahseh continued to rise, against the odds, against the world, and against the shadows that threatened to consume him.

Chapter 3

The Dark Side of Fame

With fame came the glare of a spotlight that shone too brightly, casting harsh shadows that followed Jahseh wherever he went.

The world had finally taken notice of XXXTentacion, but the attention was a double-edged sword—one side glittering with the promise of success, the other sharp with the dangers that came with being in the public eye.

Jahseh had always known that fame was a beast with a voracious appetite, devouring everything in its path—privacy, trust, even sanity. But knowing it and living it were two different things.

The demands of being in the spotlight were relentless, the pressure suffocating. Everyone wanted something from him—music, interviews, explanations—but few cared to understand the man behind the name.

The controversies that had once been whispers in the background of his life now screamed from the headlines. Legal battles loomed over him like storm clouds, threatening to engulf everything he had worked for.

The media painted him as a villain, dissecting his past with a ruthless precision, often ignoring the context that shaped his actions.

To the world, he was a complex figure—part artist, part outlaw—and the balance between the two was often lost in the frenzy of public opinion.

But it wasn't just the external pressures that weighed on him.

Jahseh's inner demons were relentless, clawing at the edges of his mind, pulling him into dark places that he struggled to escape.

The fame that had once seemed like a dream was quickly becoming a nightmare, and the lines between reality and the persona he had created began to blur.

His relationships bore the brunt of this turmoil. Friends he had once trusted grew distant, either pushed away by the intensity of his life or seduced by the temptations that came with being close to fame.

Romantic relationships, too, were fraught with tension—love, for Jahseh, was both a refuge and a battlefield, a place where he could be vulnerable, but also where he was most exposed to hurt.

In the quiet moments, when the noise of the world faded and he was left alone with his thoughts, Jahseh wrestled with questions that had no easy answers.

Was the price of fame worth the toll it was taking on his soul? Was he destined to be remembered for his music, or for the mistakes that had become public spectacles? And most hauntingly, would he ever find peace in a world that seemed determined to deny it to him?

Yet, even in the darkest moments, there was a spark within him that refused to be extinguished.

Music remained his lifeline, a way to channel the chaos inside him into something that could be understood, something that could connect him to others who felt the same pain.

His music began to evolve, taking on new depths, new layers of emotion that reflected the complexity of his life. Songs like "Jocelyn Flores" and "17" became windows into his soul, revealing a young man who was grappling with loss, regret, and the weight of his own actions.

He didn't shy away from the darkness—instead, he embraced it, using his music as a way to explore the parts of himself that the world didn't see.

For his fans, this honesty was a lifeline of their own, a reminder that they weren't alone in their struggles, that even someone who seemed larger than life could feel the same pain, the same doubts.

But the darkness was never far away. As his music
reached new heights, so too did the shadows that clung
to him. The pressures of fame, the constant scrutiny, and
the unresolved pain of his past began to take their toll.
Jahseh was caught in a cycle of highs and lows, moments
of clarity followed by periods of deep despair.

Despite it all, Jahseh continued to push forward, driven
by a relentless need to create, to leave something behind
that would outlast the chaos of his life. He was
determined to make his mark on the world, to be more
than just another name in the headlines. But with every
step he took, the path became narrower, the light at the
end of the tunnel more elusive.

And as the world continued to watch, waiting for him to either rise or fall, Jahseh Onfroy—XXXTentacion—faced the darkest parts of himself, knowing that the battle was far from over.

He was on a journey that few could understand, a journey that was as much about survival as it was about success. And in the end, it was a journey that would test him in ways he could never have imagined.

Chapter 4

MUSIC AS THERAPY

In the chaotic world Jahseh inhabited, music was his only constant, the one thing that made sense when nothing else did. It was his therapy, a way to make sense of the thoughts and emotions that raged within him.

Each beat, each lyric, was a way to exorcise his demons, to transform his pain into something tangible, something that could be shared with the world.

The success of "17," an album that laid bare the depth of his struggles, marked a turning point. It was a raw, unfiltered glimpse into the mind of a young man who was both haunted by his past and desperate to find a way forward.

Songs like "Jocelyn Flores" and "Everybody Dies in Their Nightmares" resonated deeply with listeners who found in them a reflection of their own pain and despair.

The album wasn't just music—it was a lifeline for those who felt lost, a reminder that they weren't alone in their suffering.

For Jahseh, the creation of "17" was an act of survival. It was an album born out of necessity, a way to process the grief, guilt, and self-doubt that threatened to overwhelm him. The recording sessions were intense, emotional experiences that left him drained but also brought a sense of release.

In the studio, he was free to express the parts of himself that he kept hidden from the world—the fears, the regrets, the moments of vulnerability that the public never saw. But music was more than just a way to cope— it was a way to connect. Jahseh's relationship with his fans was unlike anything most artists experienced.

He didn't just have followers; he had a community of people who saw in his music a reflection of their own struggles. His lyrics spoke to the outcasts, the misunderstood, the ones who felt like the world had turned its back on them.

And in return, his fans gave him a sense of purpose, a reason to keep going even when the weight of his own life felt too heavy to bear.

This connection was most evident in his live performances, where the energy between Jahseh and his audience was almost palpable.

The shows were chaotic, cathartic experiences, more like therapy sessions than concerts. Fans screamed his lyrics back at him, their voices blending into one, creating a powerful sense of unity and shared experience.

For those brief moments, the barriers between artist and audience disappeared, and they were all just people trying to make sense of their pain.

But as much as music was a source of healing, it was also a source of conflict. The more Jahseh poured into his art, the more he had to confront the parts of himself he wasn't sure he wanted to face.

His music forced him to wrestle with his past, with the mistakes he had made and the people he had hurt. It was a double-edged sword, offering both solace and a mirror to his own soul.

Jahseh's creative output was prolific, and his music began to take on new dimensions. He experimented with different genres, blending elements of rap, rock, R&B, and even acoustic sounds to create something uniquely his own.

His lyrics, once focused primarily on his personal struggles, began to explore broader themes—love, betrayal, existential dread, and the search for meaning in a world that often seemed devoid of it.

His follow-up album, "?," showcased this evolution. It was an eclectic mix of styles and emotions, a reflection of Jahseh's refusal to be boxed in by any single genre or label. Tracks like "Sad!" and "Changes" became anthems for a generation grappling with their own emotional turmoil.

The album was a commercial success, solidifying Jahseh's place as one of the most influential artists of his time.

But the success brought with it new challenges. The more popular Jahseh became, the more he felt the pressure to deliver, to live up to the expectations of his fans and the industry.

The demands on his time and energy were relentless, and the boundaries between his public persona and his private self began to blur.

Music, once a source of refuge, became another battlefield where Jahseh fought to maintain his sense of self.

Yet, through it all, he never lost sight of why he made music in the first place. It was his therapy, his way of making sense of a world that often seemed senseless. It was his way of reaching out to others who felt as lost as he did, offering them a piece of himself in the hope that it might help them find their own way.

And so, even as the world around him grew increasingly chaotic, Jahseh continued to create, to express, to connect.

His music was his legacy, the one thing that would endure long after the noise of fame had faded. In his songs, he found a way to live, to survive, and to give voice to the emotions that so many others struggled to articulate.

For Jahseh Onfroy—XXXTentacion—music wasn't just an art form. It was life itself.

CHAPTER 5

THE WEIGHT OF LEGACY

As Jahseh's music reached more ears and his influence spread, the idea of legacy began to weigh heavily on him. What would he leave behind when the music stopped? What would people remember? These questions haunted him, pushing him to think beyond the moment, beyond the fame, to something more enduring.

The pressures of building a legacy were compounded by the turbulence in his personal life. The controversies that had followed him since the beginning of his career refused to fade into the background.

Legal issues, public spats, and the scrutiny of a judgmental media landscape all threatened to overshadow his artistic achievements.

Jahseh knew that to many, he was a polarizing figure—admired by some, vilified by others.

But he was determined to redefine his narrative. He wanted to be more than just the sum of his mistakes. He started to talk openly about his desire to change, to grow, to be a better person—not just for himself, but for those who looked up to him. He recognized the power he held as a role model, and he wanted to use it to inspire positive change.

This shift in focus led Jahseh to embark on a path of self-improvement. He sought therapy, read books on philosophy and spirituality, and tried to surround himself with people who supported his vision for a better future.

The transformation wasn't easy, and there were setbacks along the way. But Jahseh was committed to the journey, believing that his past didn't have to dictate his future.

His evolving mindset was reflected in his music. The raw, unfiltered anger that had characterized his earlier work began to give way to more introspective, nuanced expressions of his inner world.

Tracks like "Hope" and "Changes" revealed a softer, more reflective side of Jahseh, a young man coming to terms with his past and striving to carve out a better path forward.

Jahseh's outreach to his fans also became more intentional. He spoke directly to them, often through social media, encouraging them to seek help if they were struggling, to pursue their dreams, and to find their own ways to rise above the challenges they faced. His messages were simple but heartfelt, and they resonated deeply with a fanbase that saw in him a reflection of their own struggles and aspirations.

Yet, even as he worked to change his life and his legacy, the shadows of his past loomed large. The media continued to focus on his legal troubles and past mistakes, often ignoring the changes he was trying to make. Jahseh understood that the world wasn't ready to forgive him easily, that redemption was a long, difficult process that would require more than just words.

In his private moments, Jahseh wrestled with doubts and fears about his ability to truly change. He knew that the path he was on was fraught with obstacles, both external and internal. The pressures of fame, the expectations of others, and the weight of his own history all pressed down on him, making the journey toward self-redemption feel like an uphill battle.

Despite these challenges, Jahseh remained focused on his goal. He wanted to be remembered not just for his music, but for the impact he had on the lives of others.

He dreamed of building something lasting, something that would outlive the controversies and the chaos.

He wanted to create a legacy that would inspire others to rise above their circumstances, to believe in their own potential, and to strive for something greater.

As he continued to evolve, both as an artist and as a person, Jahseh's music began to reflect the duality of his existence—the tension between his past and his future, the struggle between darkness and light. He wasn't perfect, and he knew it. But he was trying, and that effort, that determination to be better, was what drove him forward.

The weight of legacy was heavy, but Jahseh was determined to carry it. He knew that his time in the spotlight might be brief, that the world could be unforgiving. But in the end, he wanted to be remembered not just as XXXTentacion, the controversial artist, but as Jahseh Onfroy, the young man who fought against the odds to create something meaningful in a world that often seemed devoid of meaning.

And so, with each new song, each public statement, each private battle, Jahseh continued to build his legacy, brick by brick, note by note, striving to leave behind something that would stand the test of time.

CHAPTER 6

THE BATTLE WITHIN

The more Jahseh pushed forward, the more he realized that his greatest battles weren't with the world, but with himself. The inner turmoil that had fueled his creativity and defined his music was also a constant source of pain, a reminder that peace was something he had to fight for every day.

Despite his success, or perhaps because of it, Jahseh felt a growing sense of isolation. The demands of fame and the pressures of maintaining a public persona left little room for vulnerability.

He had built walls around himself, walls that protected him from the scrutiny of the outside world but also trapped him within his own mind.

The anxiety and depression that had plagued him for years were never far away, lurking in the corners of his thoughts, waiting for moments of weakness to strike.

He found some solace in his music, but even that wasn't always enough. The very act of creating could be draining, forcing him to confront the darkest parts of his soul. In the studio, surrounded by the tools of his trade, Jahseh would lose himself in the process, pouring everything he had into each track.

But when the music stopped, the silence was deafening, amplifying the fears and doubts that never seemed to go away.

Jahseh's battle within was not just about his mental health; it was also about his identity. The lines between Jahseh Onfroy, the person, and XXXTentacion, the artist, had blurred over time.

He struggled to reconcile the two, to understand where one ended and the other began.

The public saw XXXTentacion as a figure of raw emotion, a symbol of rebellion and pain, but Jahseh knew that he was more than just the persona he had created.

He was a complex individual, filled with contradictions, hopes, and fears that the world rarely saw.

This internal conflict often spilled over into his personal life. Relationships, both romantic and platonic, were fraught with tension.

Jahseh's intensity, the same quality that made him a compelling artist, could be overwhelming for those close to him. He was passionate, sometimes to a fault, and his emotions ran deep.

The people who cared about him saw the struggle, the pain that lay beneath the surface, but they also saw the goodness, the kindness that Jahseh sometimes struggled to show the world.

Jahseh knew that he needed to find balance, to find a way to coexist with his demons rather than letting them control him. He turned to meditation, to spirituality, seeking answers in places he had never looked before. The more he searched, the more he realized that the peace he sought couldn't come from external sources—it had to come from within.

But this realization didn't make the journey any easier. Jahseh's past was filled with mistakes, with moments of anger and regret that haunted him.

He wanted to change, to be better, but the process of transformation was painful and slow. There were days when the weight of his past seemed too heavy to bear, when he wondered if he could ever truly escape the shadow it cast over his life.

Yet, even in his darkest moments, Jahseh found strength in the idea of redemption. He knew that he couldn't change the past, but he believed in the power of the present, in the possibility of becoming the person he wanted to be. It was a daily battle, one that required constant vigilance, but it was a battle worth fighting.

Jahseh's journey toward self-discovery and healing was reflected in his music. His lyrics became more introspective, more focused on the themes of growth and redemption.

He wasn't just making music for his fans anymore—he was making it for himself, as a way to navigate the complexities of his own mind.

Songs like "Hope" and "Before I Close My Eyes" spoke to his desire for peace, for a sense of resolution that seemed just out of reach.

But even as he fought to find balance, Jahseh remained acutely aware of the fragility of life. He had seen too much, lost too many people, to take anything for granted. This awareness gave his music a sense of urgency, a feeling that every track, every moment, mattered.

The battle within Jahseh Onfroy was far from over. It was a journey without a clear destination, a path that was as much about the process as it was about the outcome.

But with each step, with each new insight, he moved closer to understanding himself, to finding the peace that had always eluded him.

In the end, Jahseh knew that the greatest victory would not be found in fame or fortune, but in the quiet moments of self-acceptance, in the ability to look in the mirror and see not just the pain and the mistakes, but the growth, the resilience, and the strength that had carried him through.

And so, the battle within continued, a journey that was as endless as it was essential, a testament to the complexity of a life lived in the shadow of both greatness and despair.

CHAPTER 7

THE WEIGHT OF EXPECTATIONS

As Jahseh continued to navigate the labyrinth of his own mind, he became increasingly aware of the expectations that surrounded him. These expectations came from all sides—fans, the music industry, the media, and even from within himself.

Each carried its own weight, adding layers of complexity to an already intricate life.
His fans looked up to him as a voice for the voiceless, someone who articulated the pain and struggles that they themselves felt but couldn't always express.

They saw in him a beacon of hope, someone who had risen from the darkness and was trying to guide others to the light. Jahseh felt a deep sense of responsibility toward them, knowing that his words and actions carried immense influence.

He wanted to be a positive force in their lives, to offer them more than just music—to offer them guidance, support, and a sense of belonging.

But this responsibility was a double-edged sword. Jahseh knew that he wasn't perfect, that he was still grappling with his own demons. The pressure to be a role model, to live up to the image that others had of him, was overwhelming at times. He feared that he might let his fans down, that he might not be able to live up to the pedestal they had placed him on.

This fear fueled his anxiety, making him question whether he could ever truly be the person they wanted him to be. The music industry, too, had its expectations. Jahseh's success had made him a valuable asset, and there were those who wanted to capitalize on his fame. The demands for new music, for tours, for appearances, were relentless.

There was always another album to record, another concert to perform, another interview to give. The industry's insatiable hunger for content left little room for the personal growth and reflection that Jahseh so desperately needed.

He found himself torn between the desire to create on his own terms and the pressure to meet the demands of an industry that often saw artists as products rather than people.

The media's expectations were perhaps the most suffocating. Jahseh was constantly under the microscope, his every move scrutinized, his every word dissected.

The narrative that the media crafted around him was often at odds with the reality of who he was and who he was trying to become. They focused on the controversies, the mistakes, the darker aspects of his life, often ignoring the changes he was striving to make.

Jahseh felt trapped by the public image that had been created for him, struggling to break free from the labels that had been attached to his name.

And then there were the expectations Jahseh placed on himself. He was his own harshest critic, always pushing himself to do better, to be better. He wanted to evolve, to grow, to move beyond the mistakes of his past. But the journey was fraught with setbacks and self-doubt.

Jahseh often questioned whether he was capable of change, whether he could ever truly escape the shadow of his past. These internal expectations were perhaps the heaviest of all, as they were tied to his deepest fears and insecurities.

To cope with the weight of these expectations, Jahseh turned to his music once again. He used it as a way to process the pressures he felt, and to make sense of the conflicting demands in his life. His lyrics became more introspective and more focused on the themes of identity, growth, and the struggle to find one's place in the world.

He explored these ideas in songs like "Changes" and "I Don't Even Speak Spanish LOL," where he expressed the complexities of his life in a way that resonated deeply with his listeners.

But the expectations never fully went away. They were always there, lurking in the background, a constant reminder of the gap between who Jahseh was and who the world wanted him to be.

He knew that he couldn't please everyone, that he couldn't be all things to all people. But that knowledge didn't make the burden any lighter.

In his search for balance, Jahseh began to focus on the things that mattered most to him. He sought to strengthen his relationships with the people he loved, to find moments of peace and clarity amid the chaos. He also worked on accepting himself as he was, flaws and all, understanding that true growth came from within and couldn't be dictated by external expectations.

The weight of expectations would always be a part of Jahseh's life, but he was learning to carry it with grace, to let it shape him without letting it define him.

He knew that the journey was far from over and that there would be more challenges ahead. But he also knew that he was not alone, that he had the strength to keep moving forward, even when the road was difficult.

And so, Jahseh Onfroy—XXXTentacion—continued to walk the path he had chosen, navigating the pressures and expectations with the same determination and resilience that had brought him this far.

His journey was one of growth, of learning to live with the weight of the world while staying true to himself.

CHAPTER 8

SEARCHING FOR REDEMPTION

As Jahseh's life became increasingly entangled with the expectations and pressures that came with fame, he found himself yearning for something deeper—redemption. The concept was not new to him; it had lingered in the back of his mind, a distant dream that seemed almost unreachable.

Yet, as he continued to navigate the complex landscape of his existence, it became a focal point in his quest for meaning and peace.

Redemption, for Jahseh, was more than just seeking forgiveness for his past actions—it was about transformation, about proving to himself and the world that he could rise above his circumstances and become someone worthy of the love and admiration he received. He wanted to be known not just for the mistakes he had made, but for the changes he was striving to embody.

This desire for redemption led Jahseh to take tangible steps toward bettering himself. He reached out to those he had wronged, seeking to make amends in whatever way he could. He began to speak more openly about his mistakes, acknowledging the pain he had caused and expressing his commitment to growth.

These actions were not just about clearing his conscience—they were about building a new foundation for his life, one that was rooted in honesty, humility, and the desire to make a positive impact.

Jahseh also sought redemption through his music. He saw it as a vehicle for change, a way to communicate his journey and inspire others to embark on their own paths of self-discovery and healing. His songs became more introspective, reflecting his internal struggles and his hope for a better future.

Tracks like "Hope" and "Revenge" encapsulated his desire to rise above the negativity that had surrounded him for so long, to find peace and clarity in a world that often seemed chaotic and unforgiving.

But the road to redemption was not without its obstacles. Jahseh was acutely aware of the skepticism that many people held toward his efforts. The media and public opinion were slow to change, often casting doubt on the sincerity of his transformation.

Jahseh understood that redemption was not something that could be achieved overnight—it was a long, arduous process that required patience, perseverance, and a willingness to confront the darkest parts of oneself.

Despite the external doubts, Jahseh remained committed to his journey. He continued to educate himself, reading books on philosophy, spirituality, and self-improvement, seeking wisdom from those who had walked similar paths before him.

He began to meditate regularly, using the practice as a way to center himself and find inner peace amid the chaos of his life. These practices helped him to maintain his focus, to keep moving forward even when the road seemed uncertain.

His relationships with those closest to him also became a crucial part of his redemption journey. Jahseh made a conscious effort to be more present, more supportive, and more loving toward the people who mattered most to him. He recognized that his past behavior had strained many of his relationships, and he was determined to rebuild those connections on a foundation of trust and mutual respect.

The fans who had stood by him through thick and thin were another source of strength for Jahseh. Their unwavering support gave him the motivation to keep going, even when the odds seemed stacked against him. He saw in them a reflection of his own struggles, a reminder that he was not alone in his journey.

Jahseh knew that his redemption was not just about himself—it was about proving to his fans that change was possible, that no matter how dark things seemed, there was always a way forward.

As he continued to work on himself, Jahseh began to see glimpses of the person he wanted to become. He felt moments of peace, of clarity, of connection to something greater than himself. These moments were fleeting, but they were enough to keep him moving forward, to keep him believing that redemption was within reach.

But Jahseh also knew that the journey was far from over. Redemption was not a destination, but a continuous process of growth and self-improvement. It required constant vigilance, a willingness to face one's flaws and shortcomings, and the courage to keep pushing forward, even when the path was difficult.

In the end, Jahseh's search for redemption was not just about erasing the past—it was about building a future that he could be proud of, a future where he could look back on his life and know that he had done his best to become the person he wanted to be. It was about finding peace within himself and using his experiences to help others find their own way.

And so, Jahseh Onfroy—XXXTentacion—continued his journey, driven by the belief that redemption was possible, that he could rise above his past and create a legacy that would inspire others to do the same.

CHAPTER 9

A NEW VISION

With each step Jahseh took toward redemption, he began to develop a new vision for his life. This vision was not just about personal growth, but about using his platform to make a positive impact on the world. Jahseh had always been aware of the influence he wielded, but now, more than ever, he felt a responsibility to use it for something greater than himself.

The world he had grown up in, and the one he now navigated as a public figure, was filled with pain, violence, and inequality.

Jahseh knew these realities all too well; they had shaped his experiences and his music. But he also knew that change was possible, that even the smallest actions could ripple outward and create something better. He wanted to be a part of that change, to help others find their way out of the darkness that he had spent so much of his life battling.

This new vision took shape in several ways. Jahseh became more involved in his community, using his resources to support initiatives that aimed to uplift those in need. He donated to charities, supported programs that helped at-risk youth, and encouraged his fans to do the same. He understood that real change required collective effort, and he wanted to inspire others to join him in making a difference.

Jahseh also began to use his music as a tool for social change. He started to write songs that addressed the issues he cared about—mental health, violence, systemic inequality—using his lyrics to raise awareness and spark conversations.

He saw music as a universal language, one that could transcend barriers and reach people in ways that other mediums could not. His tracks became more than just expressions of his personal struggles; they became rallying cries for those who felt voiceless and unheard.

In interviews and on social media, Jahseh spoke openly about his desire to be a positive force in the world. He encouraged his fans to look beyond their own circumstances, to think about how they could contribute to their communities and support one another. He wanted to build a movement of positivity and empowerment, one that would continue long after his music stopped playing.

But Jahseh also knew that this new vision required him to be disciplined and focused. The challenges he faced in his personal life did not simply disappear because he had decided to change.

The temptation to fall back into old habits, the pressures of fame, and the constant scrutiny of the public eye were still very real obstacles.

Jahseh had to constantly remind himself of the reasons he had embarked on this journey in the first place, to stay true to the path he had chosen.

One of the most significant changes in Jahseh's life was his approach to mental health. He began to prioritize his well-being, recognizing that he could not help others if he did not first help himself.

Therapy, meditation, and self-reflection became key components of his daily routine. These practices helped him to stay grounded, to maintain clarity in the face of adversity, and to keep his focus on his goals.

Jahseh's relationships also evolved as part of this new vision. He sought to surround himself with people who supported his growth, who shared his values, and who would hold him accountable to the standards he set for himself.

He distanced himself from toxic influences and embraced those who encouraged him to be the best version of himself. These relationships provided him with the support he needed to stay on course, to continue pursuing his vision even when the road became difficult.

As Jahseh's new vision began to take shape, he found a renewed sense of purpose. The music he created, the actions he took, and the words he spoke were all aligned with his desire to leave a lasting, positive impact on the world. He knew that he could not change the past, but he could influence the future, and that knowledge gave him the strength to keep moving forward.

Jahseh's journey was far from over. There were still many battles to fight, both within himself and in the world around him. But for the first time in a long time, he felt that he was on the right path, that he was moving toward something meaningful, something that mattered. His vision was clear: to be a force for good, to use his platform to uplift others and to create a legacy that would inspire change.

And so, Jahseh Onfroy—XXXTentacion—continued to forge ahead, driven by a new vision and a renewed sense of purpose, determined to leave behind a world that was just a little bit better for his having been in it.

CHAPTER 10

THE SHADOW OF HIS FATHER

Jahseh's journey through life was profoundly shaped by his relationship with his father, a figure who loomed large in his memory, casting a shadow that influenced much of his emotional landscape. From a young age, Jahseh's experiences with his father were marked by a complex mix of love, admiration, disappointment, and pain—a mixture that would go on to play a significant role in the man he would become.

Jahseh's father, Dwayne Ricardo Onfroy, was a charismatic and enigmatic figure. He possessed a certain magnetism that drew people to him, a trait that Jahseh would inherit.

But with that charm came a darker side—a side that was steeped in the realities of a life lived on the margins, where survival often demanded tough choices and sacrifices. For Jahseh, his father was both a role model and a cautionary tale, a man whose presence and absence were equally influential.

Growing up, Jahseh idolized his father. In his eyes, Dwayne was larger than life, a man who could navigate the world with a sense of confidence and bravado that Jahseh deeply admired. He saw his father as a source of strength, someone who had an unshakeable belief in himself and who taught Jahseh to stand up for what he believed in, no matter the cost. These lessons would stick with Jahseh, shaping his approach to the world, his music, and his relationships.

However, Dwayne's life was fraught with challenges. His involvement in criminal activities and his frequent run-ins with the law meant that he was often absent from Jahseh's life, either physically due to incarceration or emotionally due to the lifestyle he led.

These absences left a void in Jahseh's life, a void that he struggled to fill. The young Jahseh longed for his father's guidance and approval, but was often met with disappointment and a sense of abandonment.

The absence of his father during crucial moments of Jahseh's upbringing contributed to the turbulence that defined much of his early life.

Jahseh was left to navigate a world filled with uncertainty, where the figures he looked to for stability and love were often missing or preoccupied with their own battles. This sense of abandonment, coupled with the instability of his home life, fueled the anger and resentment that would later find its way into his music.

Despite the pain caused by his father's absence, Jahseh never completely gave up on the relationship. In fact, the more his father drifted away, the more Jahseh seemed to yearn for his approval.

He sought to emulate the aspects of his father's personality that he admired, while also vowing to avoid the pitfalls that had led Dwayne down a troubled path. This duality created an internal conflict within Jahseh— one where he was constantly torn between the desire to be his own man and the deep-seated need to connect with the man who had given him life.

As Jahseh grew older and began to carve out his own identity, he grappled with the legacy his father had left behind. In many ways, Jahseh saw himself as a reflection of Dwayne—a man trying to make sense of a world that often seemed hostile and unforgiving.

This reflection, however, was also a source of fear for Jahseh. He worried that he was doomed to repeat the same mistakes, to fall into the same patterns of behavior that had defined his father's life. This fear was compounded by the parallels he saw between his own struggles with the law and the ones his father had faced.

Yet, even as Jahseh wrestled with these fears, he continued to seek out a connection with his father. Their relationship remained complicated, marked by long periods of silence and occasional bursts of reconciliation. When Dwayne was present, their interactions were often intense, filled with deep conversations and moments of bonding that Jahseh cherished. These moments were rare, but they provided Jahseh with a glimpse of the relationship he so desperately wanted—a relationship where he could be both a son and a friend.

Jahseh's music became an outlet for the complex emotions surrounding his father. In his lyrics, he often explored themes of abandonment, betrayal, and the search for identity—issues that were inextricably linked to his relationship with Dwayne.

Tracks like "Pain = BESTFRIEND" and "Carry On" delved into the emotional turmoil that Jahseh felt, offering listeners a raw and unfiltered look into his struggles. Through his music, Jahseh was able to process the pain of his father's absence and the impact it had on his life.

As Jahseh's fame grew, so too did the pressure to reconcile with his past, including his relationship with his father. The demands of his career left little time for personal reflection, but Jahseh knew that he could not fully move forward without addressing the unresolved issues that lingered between him and Dwayne. In the public eye, Jahseh often portrayed himself as confident and self-assured, but privately, he continued to grapple with the same questions that had haunted him for years: Who was he without his father? And could he ever truly escape the shadow that Dwayne had cast over his life?

In the final years of his life, Jahseh made a concerted effort to repair his relationship with his father. He reached out to Dwayne, seeking to build bridges where there had once been walls. These efforts were not always successful—old wounds were difficult to heal, and the years of distance had created a chasm that was hard to bridge. But Jahseh remained committed to the process, understanding that forgiveness and reconciliation were crucial to his own healing.

The relationship between Jahseh and his father was a defining aspect of his life—a source of both strength and pain, love and conflict. It shaped the man he became, influencing his music, his relationships, and his sense of self. While Jahseh never fully resolved the complexities of his feelings toward his father, his journey toward understanding and acceptance was a testament to his growth and his desire for peace.

In the end, Jahseh's relationship with his father was a mirror to his own life—a reflection of the struggles, the triumphs, and the unyielding quest for redemption that defined his existence.

And though the shadow of his father would always be a part of him, Jahseh found solace in the knowledge that he had done everything he could to rise above it, to forge his own path, and to create a legacy that was uniquely his own.

CHAPTER 11

THE FINAL CHAPTER

Jahseh Onfroy's life was one of contradictions, of light and darkness, of triumphs and trials. He had navigated a world that seemed determined to define him by his past, all while striving to create a future that transcended those definitions.

But on June 18, 2018, the world was reminded of how fragile life can be when news broke that Jahseh—known to millions as XXXTentacion—had been tragically killed. His death sent shockwaves through the music industry, leaving fans and critics alike grappling with the loss of a young artist whose potential seemed limitless.

Jahseh's final day began like many others. He was focused, driven, and immersed in his plans for the future. He had just left RIVA Motorsports, a motorcycle dealership in Deerfield Beach, Florida, where he was looking to purchase a new bike.

Jahseh had recently turned 20 and was in the midst of a creative renaissance, working on new music and expanding his philanthropic efforts. He was also looking forward to the birth of his first child, a son who would carry on his legacy.

But the life that Jahseh had been meticulously building was cut short in an instant. As he pulled out of the dealership's parking lot in his black BMW i8, a vehicle blocked his path.

Moments later, two men approached Jahseh's car. What happened next was a tragic and violent act that ended Jahseh's life.

He was shot multiple times in what authorities later described as a robbery.

The gunmen fled the scene, leaving Jahseh bleeding in his car. Despite the efforts of first responders, Jahseh was pronounced dead shortly after arriving at the hospital.

The news of Jahseh's death spread rapidly, first through social media and then through mainstream news outlets. Fans were in disbelief, struggling to come to terms with the sudden loss of an artist who had meant so much to so many.

Jahseh's music had provided a voice for those grappling with their own pain and trauma, and now that voice had been silenced.

Tributes poured in from around the world, as fans, fellow artists, and even those who had once criticized him expressed their sorrow and paid their respects.

For many, Jahseh's death was a stark reminder of the violence that had permeated his life. From his early years in Florida to his rise in the music industry, Jahseh had been surrounded by a world where violence was an ever-present reality.

His music often reflected this, exploring the themes of pain, anger, and survival. And yet, in the months leading up to his death, Jahseh had been striving to leave that violence behind, focusing instead on healing, growth, and creating a better future.

In the wake of his death, the circumstances surrounding the shooting became the subject of intense scrutiny. The investigation revealed that the attack was premeditated, a calculated act of brutality motivated by greed. The suspects were eventually apprehended and brought to trial, but the justice that followed did little to ease the pain of those who mourned Jahseh's loss.

Jahseh's death also sparked a broader conversation about the dangers faced by young artists, particularly those who come from marginalized backgrounds.

The music industry is often portrayed as a path to escape the hardships of poverty and violence, but for many, the reality is far more complex.

Jahseh's story highlighted the risks that come with fame, especially for those who are still trying to navigate their way out of difficult circumstances. His death was a reminder that even as artists rise to stardom, they remain vulnerable to the same dangers that have always existed in their communities.

In the months that followed, Jahseh's legacy began to take shape. His music continued to resonate with fans, who found solace in the lyrics he had left behind.

Songs like "Sad!" and "Moonlight" became anthems of mourning, capturing the emotions of a generation grappling with the loss of a voice that had spoken so directly to their experiences.

Jahseh's posthumous releases, including the album Skins and Bad Vibes Forever, offered a bittersweet glimpse into the music he had been working on before his death.

These projects were a testament to his creative spirit and the potential that had been cut short.

Beyond the music, Jahseh's impact was felt in other areas as well. His foundation, the XXXTentacion Foundation, continued the philanthropic work that Jahseh had been passionate about, supporting causes that ranged from mental health awareness to youth outreach programs.

The foundation became a way for Jahseh's family, friends, and fans to honor his memory by continuing the work he had started.

Jahseh's death also led to a reevaluation of his legacy. While his life had been marred by controversy and legal troubles, many chose to focus on the positive changes he had been making in the final years of his life.

Jahseh had been on a journey of redemption, striving to become a better person and to use his platform to inspire others. In death, that journey became an integral part of his story, a reminder that people are capable of growth and transformation, even in the face of immense challenges.

For those who knew Jahseh personally, his death was an unfillable void.

He was remembered as a complex and multifaceted individual—someone who could be both kind and difficult, who was deeply sensitive yet often struggled to express his emotions in a healthy way.

His friends and collaborators spoke of his generosity, his creativity, and his intense drive to succeed.

They also spoke of the pain he had carried with him, the battles he had fought, and the hope he had for a better future.

Jahseh's relationship with his father, Dwayne, was one of the many unresolved aspects of his life that took on new significance after his death.

Dwayne had been a distant figure for much of Jahseh's life, but in the months leading up to Jahseh's death, they had been slowly rebuilding their relationship.

Dwayne was devastated by the loss of his son, and the tragedy of their strained relationship became a poignant part of Jahseh's story. In his grief, Dwayne spoke of his pride in Jahseh's accomplishments and his sorrow at not having been there for him in the ways he should have been.

Jahseh's death forced those who loved him to confront the fragility of life and the importance of healing and forgiveness.

As the world continued to mourn, Jahseh's story became a symbol of both the promise and the peril of young stardom.

His life was a testament to the power of music to heal, to connect, and to give voice to the voiceless. But it was also a cautionary tale about the dangers that can come with fame, especially for those who are still grappling with the wounds of their past.

In the years since his death, Jahseh's legacy has continued to evolve. His music remains influential, inspiring new generations of artists who see in his work a reflection of their own struggles and aspirations.

His story has become a part of the larger narrative of hip-hop, a genre that has always been about more than just music—it's been about survival, expression, and the search for meaning in a world that can often seem indifferent.

Jahseh Onfroy's life was short, but it was full of intensity, creativity, and a relentless drive to make something of himself.

He left behind a body of work that continues to resonate, a legacy of change and redemption, and a story that reminds us all of the complexities of the human experience. In death, as in life, Jahseh remained an enigma—someone who defied easy categorization, who was as flawed as he was gifted, and who, despite all the odds, left an indelible mark on the world.

LEGACY AND REFLECTION

The legacy of XXXTentacion is a tapestry woven with threads of innovation, controversy, and raw emotional expression. His impact on music and culture cannot be understated, as he forged a path that many have followed and many more have debated. His ability to blend genres, explore dark and complex themes, and connect with a generation in a deeply personal way has left an indelible mark.

In the aftermath of his passing, the conversation around his life and work has continued to evolve. Scholars, fans, and critics have all grappled with the complexities of his legacy, often finding themselves reflecting on the contradictions that defined him. His contributions to the music industry—both in terms of style and substance—are acknowledged as groundbreaking, pushing boundaries and challenging norms.

Yet, his story also serves as a cautionary tale, highlighting the precarious balance between fame and personal well-being. His struggles with mental health, legal issues, and the pressures of celebrity life underscore the challenges faced by those in the public eye. His journey serves as a poignant reminder of the importance of addressing these issues with compassion and understanding.

As we reflect on XXXTentacion's life and legacy, we are confronted with a narrative that is both inspiring and cautionary. It prompts us to consider the ways in which we engage with and interpret the lives of those who impact us profoundly.

His story invites us to look beyond the surface and engage with the deeper truths of human experience, embracing the complexities and contradictions that define us all.

In the end, XXXTentacion's legacy is a mirror held up to our own struggles, triumphs, and aspirations. It challenges us to reflect on our own journeys and the ways in which we navigate the world. His life, with all its turbulence and triumph, remains a powerful testament to the enduring impact of art and the human spirit.

XXXTENTACION'S FINANCIAL JOURNEY

In the world of music and entertainment, financial success often comes intertwined with personal and professional challenges. For XXXTentacion, his rise to fame was accompanied by significant financial gains, but also by the complexities that such success brings.

THE ASCENT TO WEALTH

From his early mixtapes to his chart-topping albums, XXXTentacion's unique sound and controversial persona quickly captured the public's attention.

As his popularity soared, so did his earnings. His music, characterized by its emotional depth and genre-blending style, resonated deeply with a generation searching for authenticity and raw expression.

This commercial success translated into substantial financial rewards, including lucrative record deals, sold-out concerts, and a growing social media presence that further fueled his brand.

THE COST OF FAME

However, financial success did not come without its own set of challenges.

The pressures of managing newfound wealth, coupled with the demands of a high-profile career, often placed XXXTentacion at the center of complex financial and personal issues.

His journey highlights the often-hidden costs of fame, including legal battles, financial mismanagement, and the constant scrutiny of the public eye.

LEGAL AND FINANCIAL STRUGGLES

XXXtentacion's financial story is also marked by legal struggles that impacted his financial stability. His involvement in multiple legal issues, including allegations and lawsuits, created financial strain and diverted attention from his music career.

These challenges were compounded by the complexities of managing large sums of money and the pressures of maintaining a public persona.

THE IMPACT ON LEGACY

Despite these challenges, XXXTentacion's financial success played a significant role in shaping his legacy.

His ability to generate substantial income from his art allowed him to explore new creative avenues and collaborate with other artists. It also provided him with a platform to influence and inspire his fans in ways that extended beyond his music.

Yet, his financial journey also underscores the importance of understanding and managing the implications of fame. The balancing act between artistic integrity and financial success is a central theme in his story, offering valuable lessons on the intersection of creativity, wealth, and personal well-being.

REFLECTION ON SUCCESS AND STRUGGLE

As we reflect on XXXTentacion's financial journey, it becomes clear that his story is not just one of artistic achievement, but also of navigating the complex realities of success.

His experiences serve as a reminder of the multifaceted nature of fame and the importance of addressing both the opportunities and challenges it brings.

In the end, XXXTentacion's financial narrative is a poignant chapter in his overall legacy—a testament to the highs and lows of his career and the lessons learned along the way.

It offers insights into the broader implications of success and the need for thoughtful management of both personal and professional aspects of life.

EPILOGUE: THE ECHOES OF XXXTENTACION

As we conclude this exploration of XXXTentacion's life, it is essential to reflect on the profound and multifaceted legacy he has left behind. Jahseh Onfroy, known to the world as XXXTentacion, was a figure whose existence defied simple categorization. His story is one of remarkable highs and devastating lows, of artistic brilliance and personal turmoil. In examining his journey, we gain a deeper understanding of the complex interplay between fame, creativity, and personal struggle.

A LEGACY OF INNOVATION AND EMOTION

XXXTentacion's rise to prominence was fueled by his distinctive voice and innovative approach to music. His genre-blending style, characterized by raw emotion and introspective lyrics, resonated deeply with a generation seeking authenticity. He pushed the boundaries of conventional music, merging elements of hip-hop, rock, and electronic genres to create a sound that was uniquely his own. His albums and tracks not only charted but also carved out a new space in the music landscape, influencing countless artists and fans.

THE DUALITIES OF HIS EXISTENCE

Yet, XXXTentacion's life was marked by stark dualities. On one hand, he was a groundbreaking artist who connected with millions through his music. On the other, he grappled with personal demons, legal issues, and the pressures of fame. His journey illustrates the often-overlooked challenges faced by those in the limelight—the struggles with mental health, the impact of legal troubles, and the constant scrutiny that accompanies celebrity.

THE PRICE OF FAME

His financial journey adds another layer to his complex narrative. XXXTentacion's success brought substantial wealth, but it also came with significant challenges. Managing this newfound fortune, navigating legal disputes, and dealing with public perception were all part of the price he paid for fame. His financial trajectory highlights the broader implications of success and the need for effective management and support systems.

IMPACT AND REFLECTION

Despite the controversies and challenges, XXXTentacion's impact on music and culture is undeniable.

His ability to articulate profound emotions and experiences in his work has left an enduring imprint on his fans and the industry.

His story is a testament to the power of art to reflect and shape the human experience, offering both inspiration and cautionary lessons.

FINAL THOUGHTS

As we close this chapter on XXXTentacion's life, we are left with a narrative that is both compelling and instructive. His legacy is a tapestry woven with threads of innovation, controversy, and emotional depth. It prompts us to consider the complexities of fame and the ways in which individuals navigate the intersection of personal struggles and public success.

XXXTentacion's journey serves as a reminder of the intricacies of the human condition, the power of artistic expression, and the often-hidden challenges of living under the spotlight. His life, though marred by conflict and tragedy, offers valuable insights into resilience, creativity, and the quest for self-discovery.

In reflecting on his story, we honor not just the artist, but the human being who, through his music and his struggles, contributed to a broader conversation about the nature of success, the impact of fame, and the quest for redemption. XXXTentacion's legacy, with all its complexities, continues to resonate and inspire, inviting us to explore the depths of our own experiences and the ways in which we navigate the world around us.

COPYRIGHT

Rebel Moon: XXXTentacion's Journey Against the World
Author: LARTX

Made in United States
Troutdale, OR
10/17/2024

23848998R00060